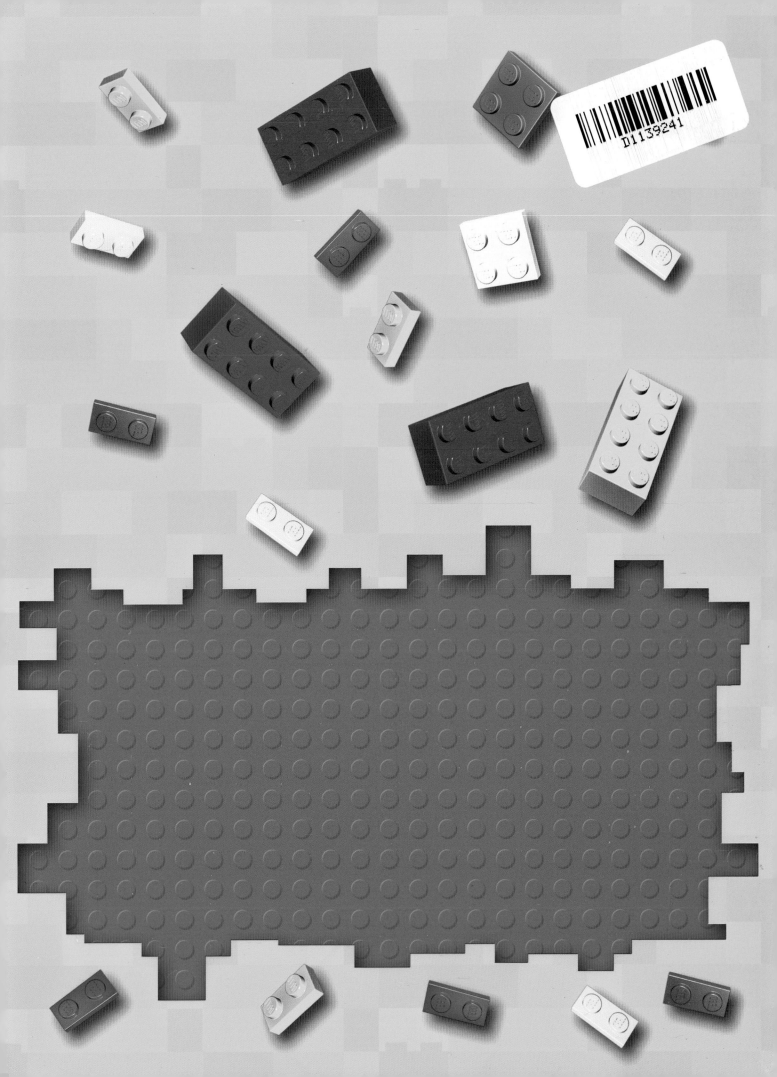

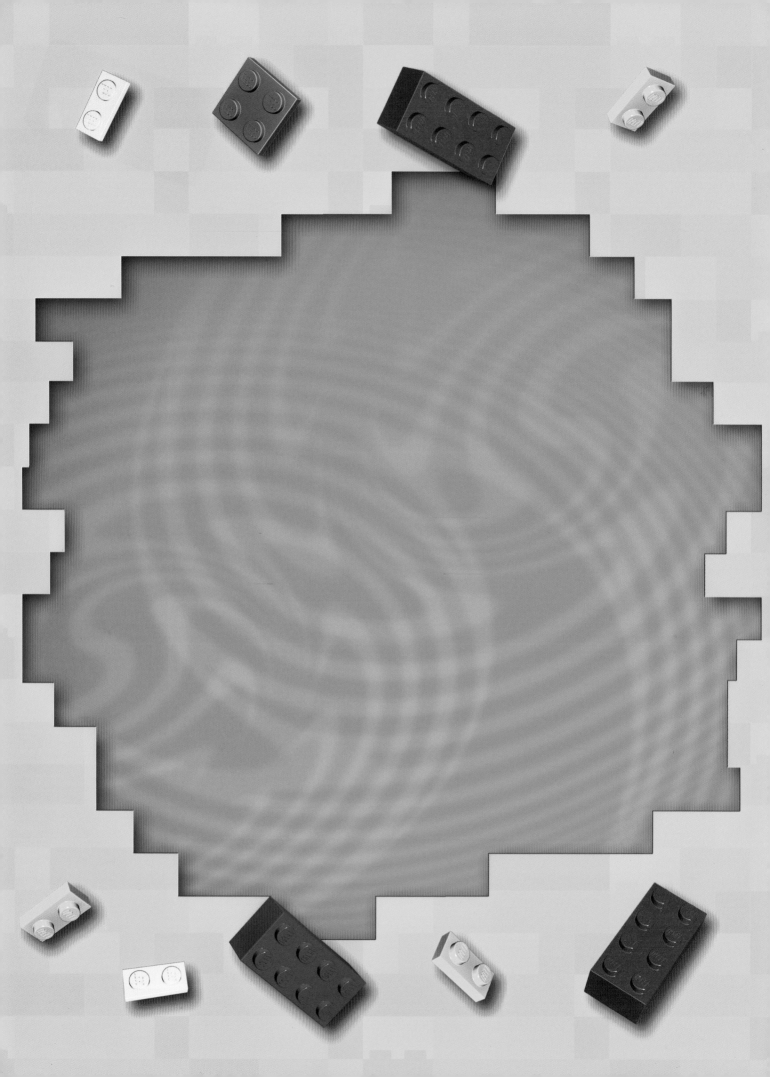

# THE OFFICIAL LEGO® ANNUAL 2016

# CONTENTS

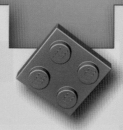

# Construction Count

This demolition crew are hard at work in LEGO® CITY! They are in a hurry to clear the area for a new building to be constructed. It's proving difficult, though, as three of the demolition workers couldn't make it to the site today. Look closely at the eight portraits below and work out who is missing.

# Thirsty Work

# A Speedy Getaway

This thief is about to get caught! The LEGO CITY Police have tracked the criminal down, along with all the money she's stolen. Work out which line will lead the helicopter to the speedboat.

# Catching the Crooks

The police have uncovered a place where thieves have been stashing stolen money. Now the thieves are trying to escape! Look closely at the six shadows below and work out which one matches the policeman's speedy hovercraft.

1

2

3

4

5

6

# Picture Pieces

The demolition crew have left a scene of destruction on this site!
Help the team out by studying the eight fragments below, then work out
which two pieces have not been taken from anywhere else in this picture.

1

2

3

19244

4

5

6

7

8

# Railway Ruckus

These construction workers have their hands full today! They need to clear this site quickly to let four trains pass. Find all the items in the box below to help them get the job done.

x2

x2

x2

x3

x3

# Spot the Difference

Who's going to catch the crook first? Will it be the nasty crocodile or the police officer in his speedy seaplane? See if you can find the five differences between these two exciting pictures!

# Tyre Trouble

This driver has had some bad luck. His car has broken down on the motorway! Luckily there's a tow truck nearby to help out. Look at the five pictures in the yellow box below and see if you can match them to the spaces in this scene.

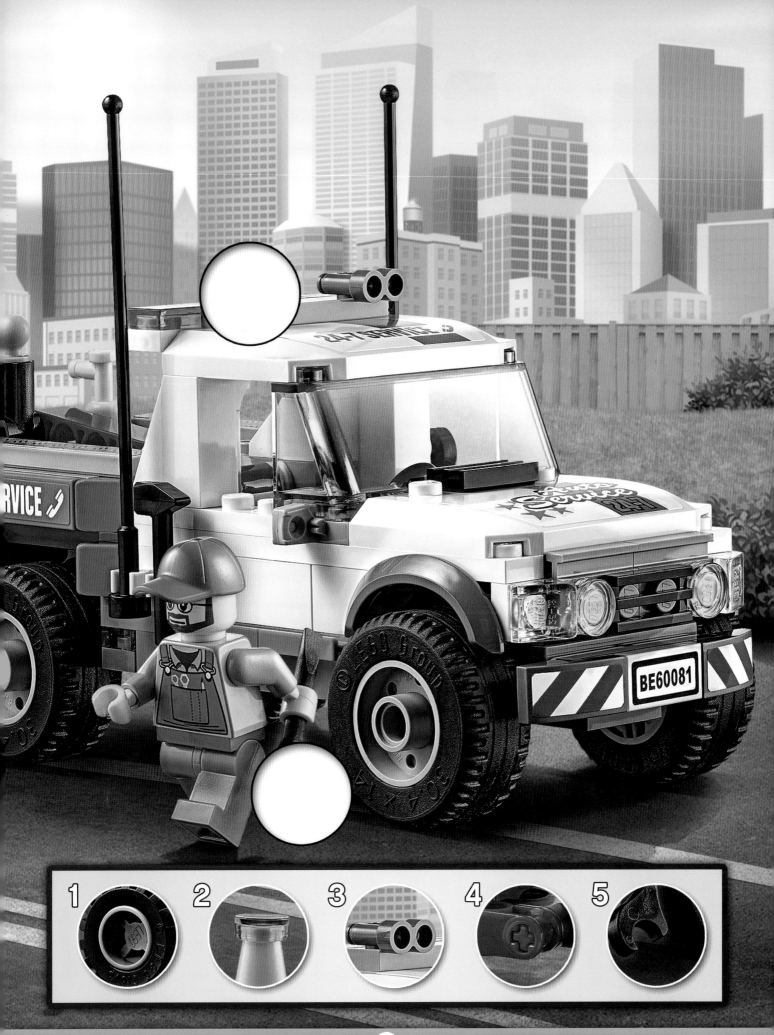

24-7 SERVICE

SERVICE

Service 24-7

BE60081

1 2 3 4 5

# Snowy Security

This snowplough needs a special activation password to get started, but the driver has forgotten what it is! Can you help him work it out from the puzzle on the right? Circle every fourth letter in this sequence, then unscramble those eight letters to work out the chilly password.

ANHWGBROPKLBPMNSKHYLSFWAJYHNBDFL

# Costume Competition

The Minifigures are having a fancy-dress party and everyone wants to win the prize for the best costume. Who have the judges chosen as the winner? Read the four clues below and see if you can work it out.

- *The winner is wearing a hat or helmet.*
- *There's a big smile on the winner's face.*
- *The winner is standing near the lifeguard.*
- *The best costume is related to food.*

Official LEGO® Annual 2016

# Dangerous Maze

The final level of the game *Labyrinth of the Night* is definitely the hardest!
Help this player complete it by drawing a path through the maze.
Make sure you avoid the poisonous snakes!

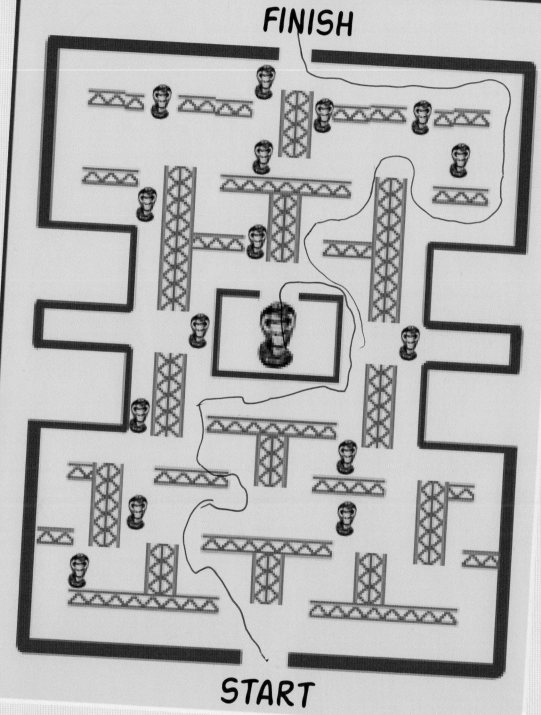

FINISH

START

# Princess Problems

THE SUN IS SHINING AND THE WIND IS BLOWING SOFTLY. IT'S SUCH A BEAUTIFUL DAY THAT THE PRINCESS HAS DECIDED TO TAKE A STROLL IN THE GARDEN.

SUDDENLY...

CROAK! CROAK!

OH, LOOK! A FROG!

# Duelling Practice

A warrior is put to the test in battle, but always makes sure to get plenty of practice first! Sharpen your logic skills by finding a friend and playing noughts and crosses with them on the grids below. Who will win? There's only one way to find out . . .

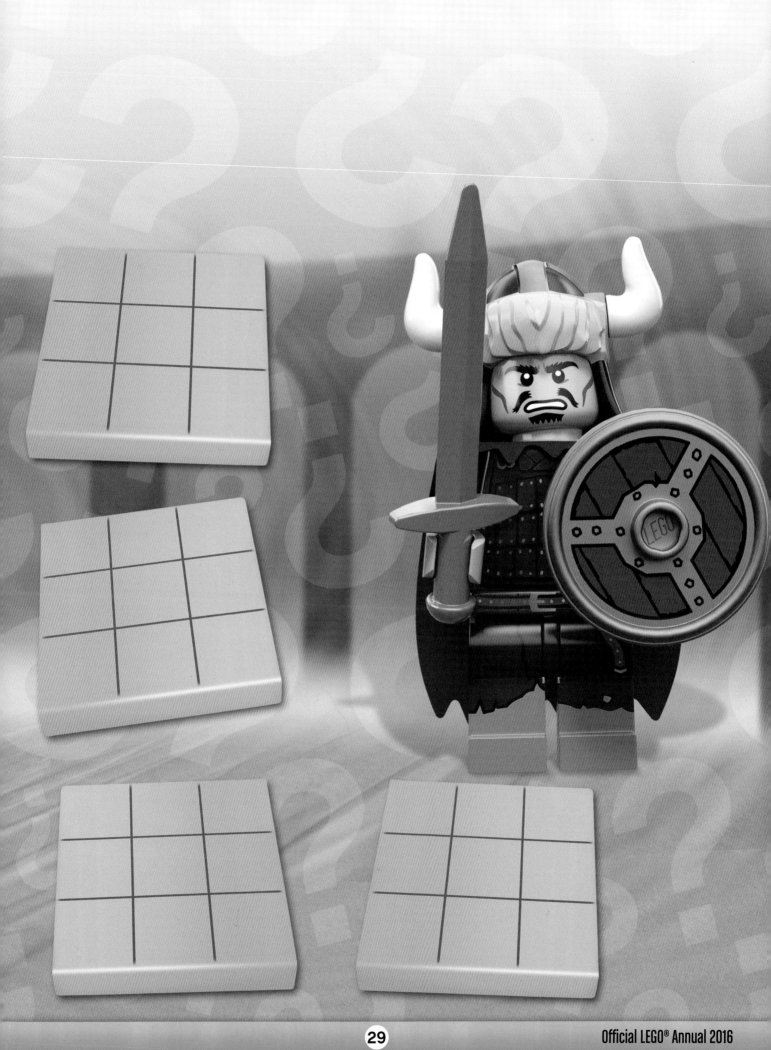

# Vampire Vision

This spooky lady is looking for her vampire friend. Unfortunately, he has turned into a bat and she is having trouble recognizing him! Can you work out which of the six bats below exactly matches the bat in her picture?

# Joker's Puzzle

The king's jester wanted to show off with a cool card trick, but he's got his cards all mixed up. Can you work out which card in each row is the odd one out?

A

B

C

# Shield Sorting

This Olympic warrior has a difficult challenge for you. Can you organize the shields by filling in the spaces with one of the four shields shown below the grid, making sure that no shield is repeated in each row or column?

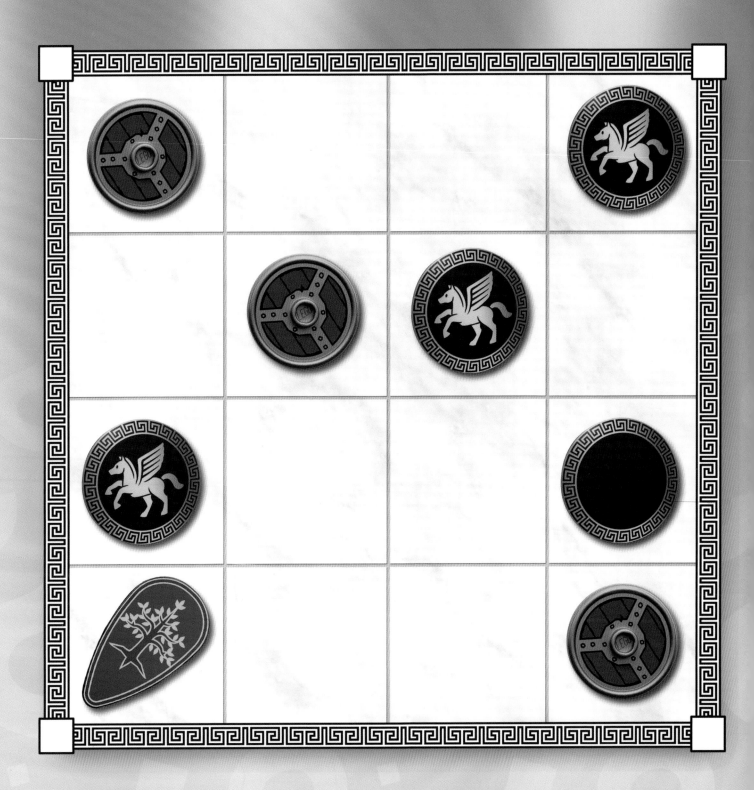

# Goblin Mischief

This goblin likes to play tricks on everybody – even this sweet kitten! The goblin has tangled up this ball of string so that the kitten can't play with it. Work out which of the three starting points will lead the kitten to its ball!

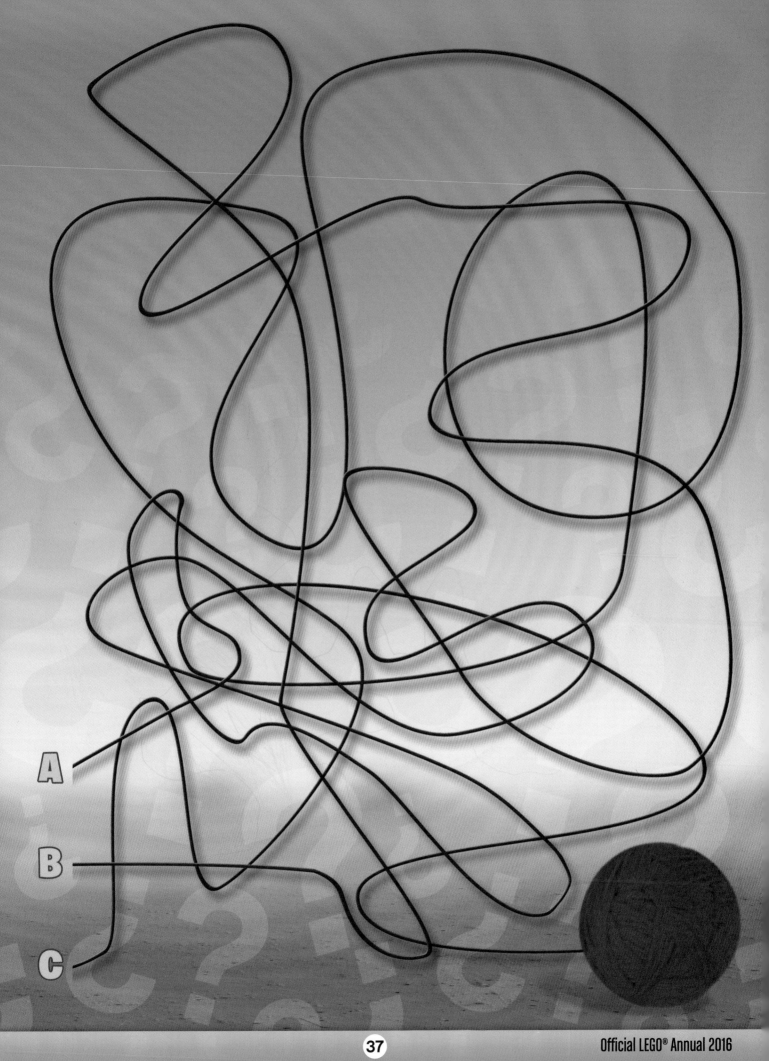

# Gold Rush

This gold miner has uncovered something very valuable. It's an old treasure map that leads to a secret stash of gold! Draw a path through the map to lead the gold miner to his bounty.

START

# Magical Mysteries

This wizard has a tricky logic puzzle for you. How many squares can you see in the drawing below? The answer might not be as simple as you think!

Number of squares:

This evil wizard uses dark magic to cast his spells. Look at the three pictures of him below, labelled A, B and C, and work out which one is his exact mirror image.

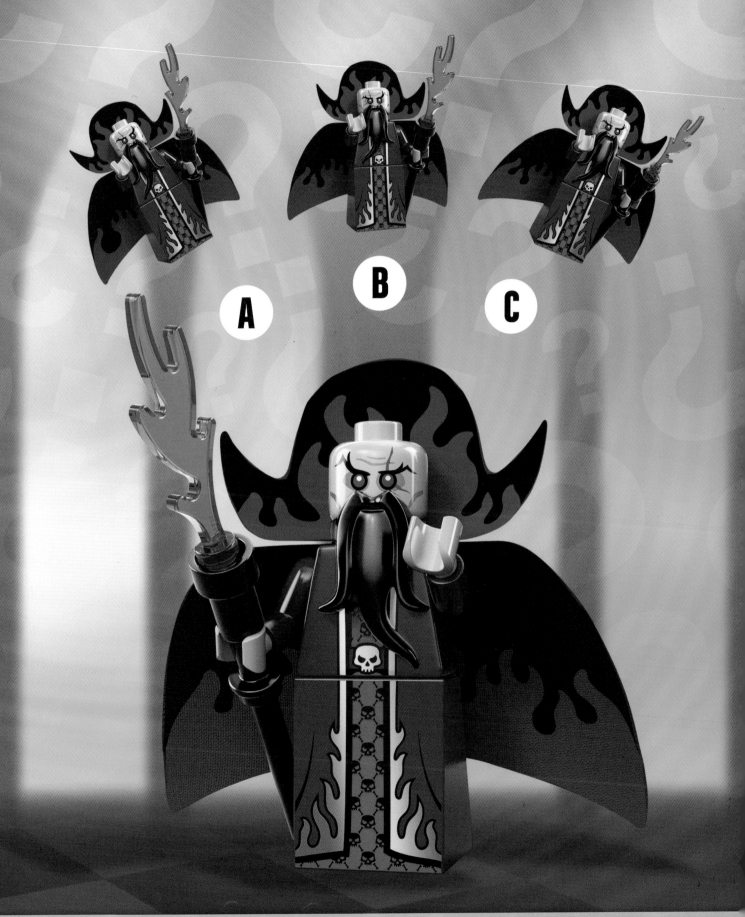

# Long Live the Pirates!

Ahoy! The captain and crew of this ship are off on an exciting journey. They aren't afraid of sea monsters or their enemies, the Bluecoat Soldiers. They're off to seek riches on the seven seas! Can you work out which of the two pictures below is an exact mirror image of the ship on the left?

1.

2.

# Land Ahoy!

CAPTAIN, WAKE UP!

LAND AHOY!

LAND? BUT WE'RE SUPPOSED TO BE...

...AT SEA!

WE JUST FOLLOWED YOUR ORDERS.

WHAT ORDERS?

THE ONES YOU GAVE LAST NIGHT.

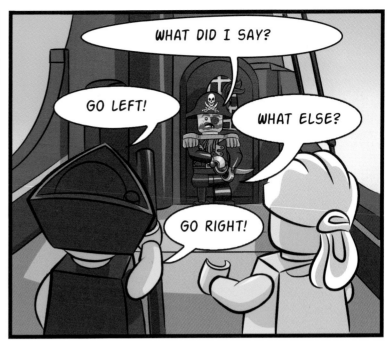

# Battle at the Fort

The fort is under attack! Whoever wins the battle will get hold of the royal treasure chest. Both sides are cunning, but the fort guards have better weapons than the sneaky pirate intruders. Can you find five differences between these two battle scenes?

Official LEGO® Annual 2016

# Treasure Island

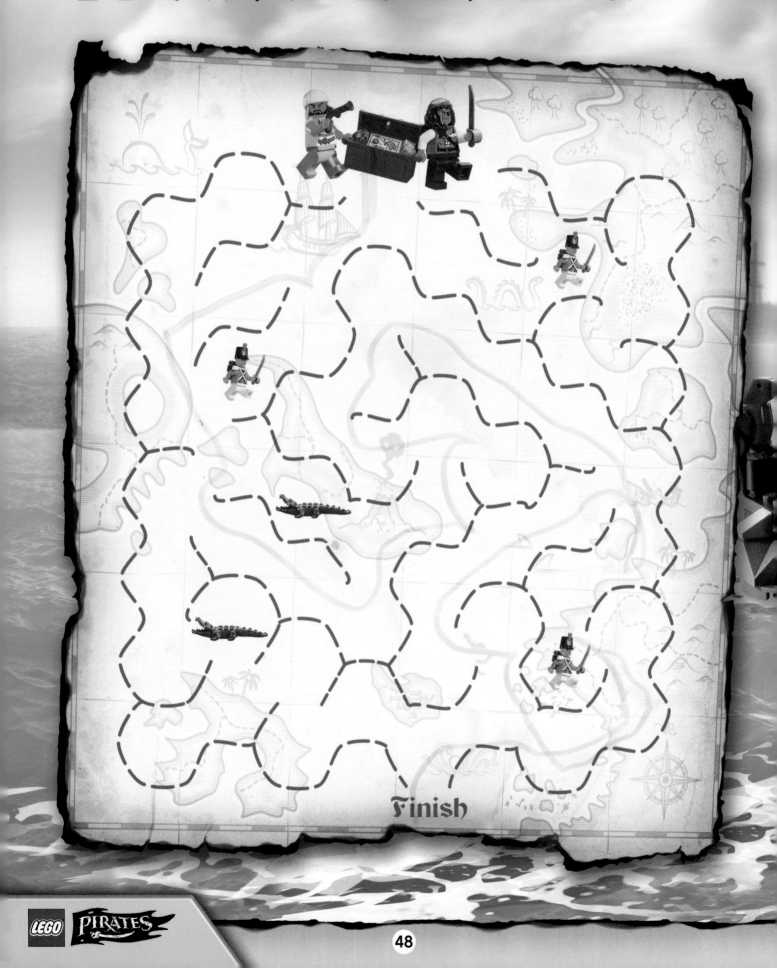

Finish

The Bluecoat Soldiers have discovered the pirates' hideout on Treasure Island! The Pirate Queen and her loyal subjects must quickly hide their treasure. Lead them through the maze so they can escape, but don't get caught by crocodiles or soldiers!

# Pirate Problems

This pirate is not having a very good day! His ship sank so he escaped on a raft, but now he is being attacked by a giant octopus and fired at by soldiers! Can you work out which of the six pictures below does not appear anywhere in this sorry scene?

# Treasure Trail

JUMP BACK!

JUMP FORWARD!

Start

LEGO PIRATES

Who will make it to the captain's treasure chests first?
Find out by playing this swashbuckling Treasure Trail game!

Find a friend to play with and choose a small object each to use as your counters. Place your counters at the start. Take it in turns to roll a dice and move your counter forward the number of spaces the dice shows. If you land on a sea creature, follow the instructions in the box below. The first player to the finish is the winner. Shiver me timbers, and may the best pirate win!

**Finish**

JUMP BACK!

Go back to the start

Move forward four spaces

Miss a turn

# Rescue Race

This pirate has been separated from his crew and is under attack! He needs help from his comrades, but which pirate will get to him first? Complete the jewel sums underneath each portrait. The pirate with the most jewels will save the day!

# Answers

## p. 4 Construction Count

2

4

7

## p. 12 Picture Pieces

1

4

## p. 8 A Speedy Getaway

## p. 14 Railway Ruckus

## p. 10 Catching the Crooks

3

## p. 16 Spot the Difference

## p. 18 Tyre Trouble

## p. 20 Snowy Security

SNOWBALL

## p. 22 Costume Competition

The winner is:

## p. 24 Dangerous Maze

FINISH

START

## p. 30 Vampire Vision

# p. 32 Joker's Puzzle

# p. 36 Goblin Mischief

# p. 34 Shield Sorting

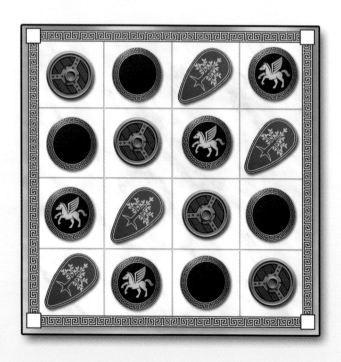

# p. 38 Gold Rush

## p. 40 Magical Mysteries

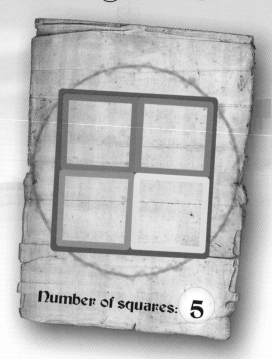

Number of squares: **5**

## p. 41 Magical Mysteries

**B**

## p. 42 Long Live the Pirates!

2.

## p. 46 Battle at the Fort

## p. 48 Treasure Island

Finish

## p. 50 Pirate Problems

## p. 54 Rescue Race

+ = 12